Snow Star

by

Martyn Hesford

Copyright © 2021 Martyn Hesford

ISBN: 9798754364820

PublishNation

Martyn Hesford is a BAFTA-nominated screenplay writer, theatre playwright and poet. His film screenplays include FANTABULOSA! starring Michael Sheen, and MRS LOWRY AND SON starring Vanessa Redgrave and Timothy Spall. His theatre plays have been performed at Hampstead Theatre and Trafalgar Studios London. LILAC WHITE is Martyn Hesford's first collection of poetry. THE MOON IS BLUE is his first novel.

twelve poems for winter

for my brother

Howard Hesford

1

I am walking
in a forest
of snow
stars.

I see

the glittering.

the whiteness.

the frosted mirror

the splinters of glass.

all is

the winter's night.

all is

the glittering

falling
into darkness.

the frozen earth
is spinning.

the angel is coming.

this winter ice

her mirror.

all is

the sparkle.

of

dusk.

2

the star glitter

falling
silver softly onto my head.

alone.

this night

this moment.

the hush.

I do not feel lonely.

here

I fight
the cold.

mirror shard
mirror broken

fragments

mirror splinters
mirror image

I see

in the glass

your face

in cold cold

memory.

the ghosts
of winters'

past.

you come
to me

from
far away

your name
almost
forgotten.

more visited in dreams.

I feel you
close tonight

this winter eve.

the excitement of early morning snow

a fairylight world.

I left you
at sixteen

to grow.

pushed you away.

no letters written
no phone calls made

a life of sophistication
more important
I thought to discover
something new

not really knowing
the harm
in

forgetting.

but
in moments
always knowing
I was running

running
numb

to find?

what?

something
better?

myself.

what was that?

thinking you
had
nothing
more

to give.

you

buried in the snow.

yet
still you come here
tonight

and open
that door

let me in

the whispers
heard

the remains

of
flesh and blood

snuffed out
years and years ago

the flickering
winter candle

the unappreciated
still
smiling

caring

faraway

the love.

still loved.

3

even
in blindness

you know

I am
here

still.

the light
the brightness.

the circle
of stones.

this hush.

those that see
will always see

know

by instinct

all lasts.

nothing

here

need
be

lost

nor given
away.

we pass through
the gate

together

each wearing

silver crowns.

we dance

our winter's dance.

we whisper

a holy secret.

never
step on

a moon moth's

wing.

we smile

we know

all
is purity

all
is radiant

all is
luminous.

each snowflake

melting

here

is precious.

never to be
seen
again.

and yet
never gone.

4

alone

in the forest

I see the red

the beating heart

the first lamp lit.

all this.

the coldness
of the cruel

death

in nature.

the animals sleeping
under the ground wrapped away
in crumpled dry leaves

they dream.

I dream.

I talk to the air

I feel you.

I hear the snow blowing
against the glass.

there is a fluttering.

a small little whisper.

I see nothing
when I look
to find you

but I know
you
are here.

frozen in the air
around me.

we move in the same place
constantly together.

you unseen

but heard
by me.

I feel your presence

I breathe the air

there is love

frozen in ice

in silence

behind

the glass walls.

somewhere

a little boy is lost.

alone
a man cries.

somewhere

a sparrow

is found

with

a broken

wing.

never to fly
again.

5

and yet
against the dark blue
sky

I see

each branch
glints with a little star.

the moon
is watching

through fading
sighs.

a silver
sixpence

a sparrow's eye.

blink
blink
blink.

God is

magic.

do you believe?

6

I am fading
into blue

moon blue silver.

she walks
here

invisible.

the mist her carpet

the branch of the willow her wand.

the moths have made her crown

they flutter around
her shoulders.

her face is unseen
porcelain bone white.

she is going to sleep.

the world
can never hide.
                    the drowning
branches lift themselves reaching for the sun

their arms and hands tearing
    the opening gap of daybreak.

she is singing no song.

she is mouthing her spell.

the blue
is her breath

there is no warmth

here.

she is
the winter time.

the cold
heartbeat.

the ice.

the stillness.

the frost.

a covering

of snow.

her beauty kills.

7

the robin bleeds.

a heart
pierced breast.

the ice
the mirror of cold cold breath.

in the silence

the feeding of a newborn deer.

the night owl

watches.

all.

the blood
on the white
pure
snow.

all.

life.

is

spilt.

and still
the old church bell chimes

the frayed rope
of different
hands

bringing forth

the winter ritual.

in
the crisp dark

blue

evening

up above

is the ancient symbol

the mystery.

a single bright

winter

snow star

shines.

all is
a spell.

can you see?

the invisible
angel.

waiting.

8

I remember
this holy night

the white
the snow

the church
soft
chimes.

the winter eve.

hands
feet eyes mouth
ice cold frozen

the little boy
walking away

carrying
his little suitcase

quiet
as a mouse.

nobody sees
him

no mystery
here.

the trees
the criss cross branches

the hovering moon

all
is the same
here.

on earth.

never
seeing

footmarks
melting
in the snow.

never seeing

his little lips

to kiss

the cold

cold
cold

heart of winter
warm.

he buries
his little star crown
in a stable.

the people
do not

need him

see him

love him.

only
wanting

their own kind.

to sing and dance

and
make merry
freely.

with

all

their

god

given

golden eyed
gifts.

listen
listen
can you hear?

a drunkard laughs.

9

the snow queen
kisses

the little boy

his heart
freezes

piercing

cold.

in his
soul

a small
tiny white

blossom

sleeps.

nature

remains

a seed.

a little bud

waiting

encased in ice.

10

white clean
crisp
breath

red berry cold.

the purity of your memory

the winter of that day

the coming of the deer

the ending of a year

the bird that blinks.

the sparkle

of a moment

all is

remembered

today.

long

long

long

ago.

the flowers.

the snowdrops

on this white grave.

the

long

long

long

sigh.

the cry.

the fading

into the dark blue.

dust.

11

oh little bird
on a silver branch
you are the last
heartbeat (of sorrow)
in the world
you are strong
yet so soft
your soul flutters
into the white.

12

a pressed
white flower.

the crawling
little insect.

the elizabethan kiss

in perfumed
red wax.

your fingers picking.

sewing.

a needle pricking.

tiny little
blood drops

spots

on the polished wood

like red berries.

your story

once a child here
remembered.

the little chimes.

the silver echo.

the whispers

of winter's smoke.

here

the three

winter
angels

appear.

in gold.

here

the wound

crimson

open

seeps.

slowly slowly

into the snow.

bringing

the mystery

the magic

again and again.

the constant
spell

of

the little
white flower.

in the forest

the earth is kissed

cracked frozen

until

from sleep

this enchantment
breathes

life.

the earth
is reborn.

gently
gently

softly

is

the coming

spring.

inhale.

inhale.

inhale.

all.

the golden blossoms of the sun

awake.

the Snow Angel by Martyn Hesford

Made in the USA
Las Vegas, NV
12 March 2022